101

TRUTHS ABOUT
YOUR BEST FRIEND THE
HOLY SPIRIT

MATTYSON
MEDIA

MATTHEW ASHIMOLOWO

Mattyson Media Company
P. O. Box 12961
London
E15 1UR

Bible quotes are from the King James Bible unless otherwise stated.

AMP, Amplified Bible © Copyright 1987 by the Zondervan Corporation and the Lockman Foundation.

ISBN 1-874646-14-7

Printed in England by Clays Ltd, St Ives plc

INTRODUCTION

The Holy Spirit is a real personality with intellect, emotion and will.

He is the executive of the Godhead therefore he knows and can reveal the mind of God to those who seek his friendship.

'<u>What are friends for</u>?' People often ask: Friendship with the Holy Spirit means communion, direction, intimacy and depth in the things of God.

'<u>What are friends for</u>?' Ask your friend to walk with you, talk to you and take you into the depth of the Father's will.

'<u>What are friends for</u>?' This is one friend who will pray, sing, speak and help needy people through you.

Truly, he is your greatest and best friend.

1   The Holy Spirit is God's solution to
     your need of perpetual counselling.
     John 14: 16 (Amp); Jeremiah 32: 19

     ➤   His counsel is deeper and greater.

     ➤   His counsel is wise. Proverbs 24: 6

     ➤   His counsel is perfect. Job 12: 13

2   He is your ever present help in the
     time of need. John 14: 16 (Amp);
     Psalm 46: 1 Our well proved help.

3   The Holy Spirit is the best defence
     counsel you could ever have to argue
     your case.

> ➤   Defends you in love. Isaiah 4: 5, 16

> ➤   Your defence from earthly attack.
>   Psalm 94: 22

4   He is our perpetual intercessor praying
     always for you. John 14: 16 (Amp);
     Romans 8: 27; Psalm 139: 1 - 2

> ➤   To pray perfectly.

> ➤   To pray in the will of the Lord.

> ➤   To possess the future, before it
>   comes.

5   The purpose of His coming is to befriend you. John 14:16 (Amp)

6   Divine energy is yours because of this fellowship. John 14:16 (Amp)

    ➤   To be an able witness.

7   He is the standby to respond to major and minor challenges.
John 14:16 (Amp)

8   He is the Spirit of Truth sent to

➤   Protect you from error.

➤   Set you free.

➤   **Bring balance where facts are against you. John 14: 17**

9   He helps us to know, recognise and welcome the mind of God.
John 14: 17

10 Friendship with the Holy Spirit exposes you to the One who has power to act fully on behalf of Jesus. John 14: 27

11 He is here to remind you of all things, secular or spiritual, intended for your well-being. John 14: 26

12 A true understanding of Jesus is only possible as you befriend the Holy Spirit. John 16: 7

13 The Holy Spirit will befriend you and continue to remind you of your right standing in God. John 16: 8

14   Your friend is the embodiment of truth, when He leads you - you will not fall into error. John 16: 13

15   Friendship with Him will lead to intimacy with the Father. John 16: 13

> ➤   Intimacy deepens relationship.

> ➤   Intimacy results in reproduction.

16   Access into heaven's conversation is possible as you walk with your new Friend. John16: 13

17   Divine revelation is needed to walk in the light - your heavenly Friend will keep you informed. John 16: 13

18   True and deep worship is possible as the Holy Spirit leads us to the Father's presence. John 16: 14

19 You will not walk in the dark
    concerning the future - your Friend is
    from the future. John 16: 13

20 Continuous supply of heavenly
    manna, ideas, purposes come to you
    from the Father, through His
    mouthpiece on earth - the Holy Spirit.
    John 16: 14

21 You can only possess your inheritance in Christ as the Holy Spirit leads you into full possession. John 16: 15

22 Intimacy with this Friend frees us from the impact of the guilt feeling of our past lives. Romans 8: 1

23 The Holy Spirit introduces His own programme and principles to counter what has dominated us before. Romans 8: 2

24 Before He came, we were dominated by our nature, now that He is here, He takes over and helps you live on a higher dimension. Romans 8: 4

25 Friendship and intimacy with the Holy Spirit make you desire only what pleases Him. Romans 8: 5

26 To fail to befriend the Holy Spirit is to expose yourself to living by natural sense, reason and end up in misery and spiritual death. Romans 8: 6

27 The in-dwelling Spirit is the mark of our new life in Christ. Romans 8: 9

28   A focus on the Holy Spirit dwelling in you, will bring health to your physical body. Romans 8: 11

29   Intimacy with the Holy Spirit will mean starvation for your carnal nature. Romans 8: 13

30 Responding to the Holy Spirit, by saying yes to the things He wants, lifts you to the position of matured sons. Romans 8: 14

31 Total freedom from every bondage is possible through the Holy Spirit. Romans 8: 15a

32 The true depth of our sonship and the meaning of the Fatherhood of God, is only grasped through the inspiration of the Holy Spirit. Romans 8: 15b - 16

33 Life in the Holy Spirit is a foretaste of the future of blissful living.
Romans 8: 23

34 Your limitations become insignificant in the presence of the Holy Spirit. Romans 8: 26

35 The deepest depth of intercession can only be reached through the help of the Holy Spirit. Romans 8: 26b; Jude verse 20

36 Walking and living in the Spirit is the answer to living according to the domination of the flesh. Galatians 5: 16

37 Friendship with the Holy Spirit guarantees the presence of His "Fruitful qualities". Galatians 5: 22

38 The presence of the Holy Spirit produces the fruit of unconditional love. Galatians 5: 22; Romans 5: 5

39 The presence of the Holy Spirit
    brings the capacity for a gladness of
    heart not produced by temporal goods.
    Galatians 5: 22

40 Friendship with the Holy Spirit helps
    you enjoy a tranquillity of mind,
    beyond human comprehension.
    Galatians 5: 22; Philippians 4: 7

41 The in-dwelling presence of the Holy
    Spirit is the answer to handling a
    pressure cooker world without
    blowing "your top". Galatians 5: 22

42 Friendship with the Holy Spirit opens
    the hardest of us to flowing with the
    "milk of kindness". Galatians 5: 22

43   Through you, the Holy Spirit can touch many others, as you walk and show benevolence. Galatians 5. 22

44   The Holy Spirit gives the ability to stay true and be committed to the purpose of God. Galatians 5: 22

45 The world delights in relating to those who are truly humble and meek:

> ➢ Only the Holy Spirit can produce this virtue without measure.
> **Galatians 5: 23**

46 The key to self-control is not *self*, but the Holy Spirit producing the ability to walk in self-restraint and constraint. **Galatians 5: 23**

47 You can operate in supernatural knowledge of the past, present and future through your relationship with the Holy Spirit. 1 Corinthians 12: 8

48 Divine understanding into impossible situations and the wisdom to bring solution is a gift of the Holy Spirit. 1 Corinthians 12: 8; Job 32: 8

49 Friendship with the Holy Spirit gives you access to the wonder working power of the Holy Spirit.
1 Corinthians 12: 9

50 Openness and relationship with Him makes extraordinary power available to minister divine healing.
1 Corinthians 12: 9

51 Through the Holy Spirit you can
    move in the gift of miracles.
    1 Corinthians 12: 10

52 The ability to see into the past and
    predict the future become possible
    when friendship is built with the Holy
    Spirit. 1 Corinthians 12: 10

    ➢   This gift helps you to make sense
        of God's will and purpose.

53 In a world of falsehood and deceit, the Holy Spirit will give you the ability to discern what kind of spirit and motive is in operation. 1 Corinthians 12: 10

54 Friendship with the Holy Spirit becomes deeper as you speak the language He gives.
1 Corinthians 12: 10

55   Speaking the language of the Holy Spirit results in your spirit being built up. 1 Corinthians 14: 4; Jude verse 20

56   Speaking the language of the Holy Spirit exposes you to secret and hidden truths of God.
1 Corinthians 2: 9 - 10;
1 Corinthians 14: 2

57 Friendship with the Holy Spirit and speaking His language, gives you direct access to the Father.
1 Corinthians 14: 2; 1 Corinthians 2: 11

58 When the Holy Spirit prays through you, in His own language, He bypasses your human understanding.
1 Corinthians 14: 14; James 1: 8

59 Speaking the language of your
    Friend, the Holy Spirit, means you
    can let Him pray through you.
    1 Corinthians 14: 14; Romans 8: 26;
    Revelation 1: 10

60 The Holy Spirit has a beautiful
    language He does not only want to
    speak, but sing through you.
    1 Corinthians 14: 15; Ephesians 5: 19

61 The Holy Spirit is from the future, so
His language is the best for giving
God the highest praise.
1 Corinthians 14: 15; Ephesians 5: 19

62 Friendship with the Holy Spirit means
He is able to refresh and renew you in
moments of physical and spiritual
burnout. Romans 8: 27; Isaiah 28: 12

63 Friendship with the Holy Spirit is the key to full surrender of your tongue to the Holy Spirit. Ephesians 4: 29; 5: 4; Isaiah 30: 15

64 Deeper relationship with the Holy Spirit and the speaking of His language, shuts you out of worldly pressure. 1 John 2: 15

65 Praying in the language of the Holy
    Spirit helps to avoid doubting what
    you are asking for. 1 Corinthians 14: 15;
    Mark 11: 23

66 The human spirit fails, unless the
    Holy Spirit fills. Acts 4: 8

67 Divine ability, efficiency and might,
    follows the incoming of the Holy
    Spirit. Acts 1: 8

68 The in-dwelling Holy Spirit is the
    mark of God's approval.
    Ephesians 4: 30

69 The in-dwelling Holy Spirit is the
    foretaste of our inheritance.
    Ephesians 1: 14

70 In maintaining friendship with the
Holy Spirit, it is important to avoid
whatever offends, vexes or saddens
Him. Ephesians 4: 30

71 Friendship with the Holy Spirit
protects you from being frivolous
with words. Job 32: 18

72 The Holy Spirit is the only Friend who can be everywhere, every time, with you. Psalms 139: 7 - 10

73 Friendship with the Holy Spirit exposes your mind to wisdom and creativity. Exodus 31: 3; 35: 31

74 The in-dwelling presence of the Holy
Spirit will result in you being led into
that which is right. Psalm 143; 10

75 Friendship with the Holy Spirit opens
you to the power He gives to
proclaim God's Word. Isaiah 61: 1

76 Friendship with the Holy Spirit makes Him fill you with the desire to help the meek, the afflicted and the brokenhearted. Isaiah 61: 1

77 Relationship with the Holy Spirit makes available His presence and power without measure. John 3: 34

78 Relationship with the Holy Spirit makes available the yoke destroying and burden removing power of God. Isaiah 10: 27

79 The Holy Spirit is able to lift you and take you to heights you have never been before as you commune with Him. Ezekiel 3: 14

80   The key to operating with an
     excellent spirit is relationship with the
     Holy Spirit. Daniel 5: 12; 6: 3

81   The holy Spirit is able to strengthen
     you so that you can move and do
     things in His power. Luke 4: 14

82 Friendship with the Holy Spirit means
He supplies a continuous dosage of
spiritual zeal. Acts 18: 25

83 The profound and bottomless things
of God, the divine counsels and
hidden things beyond human scrutiny,
are made available through the insight
the Spirit gives.
1 Corinthians 2: 10 (Amp)

84 Intimacy with the Holy Spirit will transform you from one controlled by the spirit of fear because the Holy Spirit will give you power, love, calm and balance. 2 Timothy 1: 7

85 The in-dwelling presence of the Holy Spirit makes you God's hallowed, special residence. 1 Corinthians 6: 11

86   The Holy Spirit is the "Spirit of glory".
     His presence in you provokes satan's
     abuse, but you are blessed and highly
     favoured. 1 Peter 4: 14

87   The presence of the Holy Spirit
     brings you into the favour you do not
     deserve. Zechariah 12: 10

88 Friendship with the Holy Spirit produces supernatural knowledge. Isaiah 11: 2

89 When the Holy Spirit resides in you, He produces reverence and obedient fear of the Lord. Isaiah 11: 2

90 Spiritual birth is only possible when it is orchestrated and conducted through the Holy Spirit. John 3: 5

91 The in-dwelling presence of your
    Friend, the Holy Spirit, is the basis
    for true, deep and genuine worship.
    John 4: 23 - 24

92 When the Holy Spirit lives in you, He
    becomes a well of living, satisfying
    water, to quench your spiritual thirst.
    John 14: 14

93   The friendship you develop with the Holy Spirit makes His presence go beyond a well of truth, to become the rivers of living water. John 7: 37 - 3

94   In maintaining friendship with the Holy Spirit, do not promise to yield what you are not willing to surrender. Acts 5: 3 - 4

95　The love of the Holy Spirit is intense, therefore avoid whatever suppresses or subdues His flame in your life.
1 Thessalonians 5: 19

96　Intimate friendship with the Holy Spirit makes Him rise to defend us in the face of the devil's worst attack.
Isaiah 59: 19

97 Friendship and intimacy with the Holy Spirit, opens you to receiving open visions from Him. Joel 2: 28; 1 Samuel 3: 1

98 The in-filling presence of the Holy Spirit makes the difference. When He is allowed in, He marks you out for recognition. Joel 2: 29

99 Friendship with the Holy Spirit will help you to keep your visions and dreams alive. Joel 2: 28

100 The in-dwelling presence of the Holy Spirit makes perpetual power available. Ephesians 3: 20

101 The abilities of your friend the Holy
Spirit is revealed in his names.
Isaiah 11: 2 - 3

NAMES OF THE HOLY SPIRIT

➢ THE SPIRIT OF THE LORD

Friendship with the Holy Spirit helps you to understand and submit to the Lordship of Jesus Christ.

➢ THE SPIRIT OF WISDOM

The Holy Spirit is the spirit of wisdom, helping us to apply the wisdom of God. Isaiah 11: 2; Proverbs 2: 10 - 11

➤ THE SPIRIT OF UNDERSTANDING

Friendship with the Holy Spirit exposes us to spiritual understanding.

➤ THE SPIRIT OF COUNSEL

Friendship with the Holy Spirit makes him reveal his ability to counsel us. Isaiah 11: 2

➢ THE SPIRIT OF MIGHT

Your friend the Holy Spirit, is the spirit of might.

➢ THE SPIRIT OF KNOWLEDGE

Friendship with the Holy Spirit opens you to the deeper knowledge available through the Holy Spirit.

> ## THE SPIRIT OF THE FEAR OF THE LORD

Friendship with the Holy Spirit helps you to understand and live with reverence to the Lord.

THE VISION OF MATTYSON MEDIA

Mattyson Media is committed to the publishing of books, production of videos and audios that promote primarily the works of its founder, Rev Matthew Ashimolowo and also the products of various publishing companies which it represents.

It is our vision to use every media to make the word of God available to mankind.

We are committed to the full gospel/charismatic message and therefore it reflects in our publishing as well as distribution.

Equipping the local church with the Word. Playing our part in raising and strengthening leaders.

Touching lives with timeless truth.

Matthew Ashimolowo
Chief Executive Officer

AUDIO TAPES BY THE AUTHOR

1. Breaking Free from Generational Curses 1 & 2
2. Sing, oh Barren - Giving Thanks
3. Believers Authority
4. Taking Care of Business
5. Reality of Financial Dominion 4
6. Eagle Believer 1 & 2
7. How to Pray With Confidence
8. The Devil is a Liar 1, 2 & 3
9. What to do at the Bus Stop Called Lion's Den 1 & 2
10. The Anointing for Signs and Miracles
11. The Gift of the Spirit
12. Living Wise in the Seasons of Life - Diligence
                                    - Be Different
13. Divine Principle for Winning in Life 2
14. Evidences of Miracle Living
15. Seven Seasons of a Man's Life
16. Victory through Corporate Warfare
17. Hindrances to Spreading the Gospel
18. Secrets of Abundance 1 & 2
19. Being Different in a World of Duplicates
20. Love - the Winning Way - Importance of Self Worth
21. Walking in Love - How to fix Broken Relationships
22. Making that Change
23. Developing the Mind of Christ
24. Living on a Double Dose
25. Developing a Servant's Heart 1 & 2
26. The Sound of Triumph
27. Growing in the Grace of Jesus Christ
28. The Realm of the Spirit
29. The Making of Champions
30. From Trial to Triumph
31. From Curses to Breakthrough
32. Lazarus Generation
33. New Beginning
34. Petitioning God
35. Leaving Yesterday's Mistake Behind
36. Principle for Divine Increase 1 & 2
37. Dominion
38. The Happiest people on Earth
39. The Shout of Victory
40. How to Ride the Storms
41. Power of Attorney
42. From Pit to Palace
43. Victory Over Financial Setback
44. From Problem to Solution
45. Power of Positive Confession

46. Wisdom for Living in '94
47. Why Bad Things Happen to Good People
48. The Making of a Miracle - The Birth of Jesus
                                   - Can You Believe It
                                   - Say the Right Thing
49. No Name, No Fixed Address
51. The Journey of Faith 1 & 2
52. Singing Songs or Hanging Harps
53. Mandate of a Champion - Fruitfulness
                             - Multiplication
                             - Dominion
54. Marks of a Champion   - People of Prayer
                           - People of Praise
                           - People of Purpose
55. Songs of a Champion   - Moving in the Power & Grace of God
                           - Overcoming Temporary Setbacks
                           - Resisting the Enemy
                           - Blessing of the Shepherd Boy
56. Song of Champions   - Preparation of Champions
57. Is There a Family in Your House 1 & 2
58. Kingdom Authority   - Kingdom Rights
                         - Keys of the Kingdom
                         - Key of the Blood
59. Excellence in Life and Ministry 1 & 2
60. Principles of Financial Excellence
61. The Struggle is Over   - Broken but Blessed
                            - Moving from Sorrow to Success
                            - Positioned for Promotion
                            - Good or Bad Times ; The Word Works
62. The Unveiling of Jesus
63. Supernatural Living - The Revelation of Jesus
                          - Supernatural Protection
                          - Blessings of the Anointing
64. The Happy Attitudes   - I Need Help
                           - I Choose to be Happy Anyway
                           - I Choose to do the Right Thing Anytime
65. 5 Blessings of the Christian Home
66. Provoking God for a Turnaround

NEW RELEASES BY MATTHEW ASHIMOLOWO

➤ THE POWER OF POSITIVE PRAYER

It is a vital tool for prayer co-ordinators who lead others. There are people who would rather make positive confessions on matters raised within the book is intended for the man or woman who wants to pray but sometimes comes short of prayer points.

It is relevant for believer's need because it addresses:

- *2,000 Prayer Points*
- *50 Prayer Topics*
- *1,000 Relevant Scriptures*
- *10 Ways to get Heaven's Attention*
- *Daily Positive Confession*

➤ THE POWER OF POSITIVE CONFESSION

(Powerful Confessions for Daily Victory!)

Since words are such powerful tools;

- *Use your word to build your spirit-man*
- *Use them to paint the picture of your desired future*
- *Use them to re-write the negatives written into your life*
- *Use words to lift yourself from defeat to victory*

It is a collection of bible-based confessions written in a style that turns problems into challenges and situations inot solutions. It is based on topics in the Book 'The power of Positive Prayer'.

BOOKS BY MATTYSON MEDIA

1.) Matthew Ashimolowo

➤ ## KEEPING YOUR DREAMS ALIVE

How To Fulfil Your God Given Vision

In this book we will attempt to look at your God given dreams, visions, abilities and how you may achieve them. It will be sad to get to eternity and find that you have spent almost all your life fulfilling other people's expectationd and desires for you, while God's original purpose lies unfulfilled.

➤ ## TAKE A GIANT LEAP

(How to motivate yourself for a successful Christian Life)

➤ ## WARRIORS OF RIGHTEOUSNESS

(Occupy your place for the battle of the End Times)

➤ ## TONGUES OF FIRE

(12 Reasons for Speaking in Tongues ... and More)

➤ ## THE MAKING OF CHAMPIONS

(Developing the Lifestyle for Daily Victory)

➤ ## IT'S NOT OVER 'TILL IT'S OVER

(Keeping Your Dreams Alive)

2.) Tunde Bakare

➤ **THE CREATION OF VALUE**
➤ **OPERATING IN HIGH FINANCES**

3.) Ayo Oritsejafor

➤ **WALKING IN UNITY**

CONTACT ADDRESSES

Mattyson Media Christian Book market
8 Atinuke Atobajaiye Avenue
Off Okota Road - Okota
Celestial Bus Stop
Oshodi - Mile Two Expressway
Isolo-Lagos
Nigeria

Telephone:- 01 820 918, 526 957

Mattyson Media Christian Book market
22 Ikorodu Road
Jibowu
Lagos
Nigeria
Telephone:- 01 526 957

Kingsway International Christian Centre
1 Darnley Road
(Off Mare Street)
Hackney
London
E9 6QH

Telephone: 0181 525 0000
Facsimile: 0181 525 0002

PETITIONING GOD IN PRAYER

NAME (MR & MRS, MR, MRS, MISS):
_____

ADDRESS:
_____
_____

TOWN:
_____
COUNTY: _____ POST CODE: _____
PHONE (H): _____
(W): _____

Let us join our faith with yours for your prayer needs, Fill out the space below and send to the address given

YOUR PETITION

1. _____
2. _____
3. _____
4. _____
5. _____
6. _____
7. _____
8. _____
9. _____
10. _____

MAIL TO:-

Kingsway International Christian Centre

1 Darnley Road, Off Mare Street, Hackney, London, E9 6QH.

If you want prayer immediately, call HOPELINE on **0181 525 0000**

PERSONAL DETAILS

NAME (MR & MRS, MR, MRS, MISS): _____

ADDRESS: _____

TOWN: _____

COUNTY: _____ POST CODE: _____

PHONE (H) _____

(W) _____

FOR YOUR INFORMATION

❑ Please send me your free quarterly magazine KINGSWAY DIGEST,

❑ Please put me on your mailing list,

❑ Please send me a catalogue of Pastor Matthew's tapes and books.

MAIL TO:-

Kingsway International Christian Centre

1 Darnley Road, Off Mare Street, Hackney, London, E9 6QH.